# HOW TO GO
# CLUTTER FREE

# TIDYING TIPS FOR BUSY PEOPLE

### CAROLINE JONES

D1647603

Published in 2020 by Welbeck
An imprint of the Welbeck Publishing Group
20 Mortimer Street
London W1T 3JW

A CIP catalogue for this book is available from the British Library.

ISBN 978-1-78739-452-0

Printed in China

10 9 8 7 6 5 4 3 2 1

# CONTENTS

# INTRODUCTION

-----------------------------------

This book is here to help you on an important journey. It's a practical guide to getting rid of any unnecessary physical and psychological baggage that is holding you back.

A simpler, more streamlined life is not just about seeing how little we can get by with, or how much we can throw out, but learning to identify and ditch the excess, creating more space for you to use what is truly vital more efficiently and more joyfully.

Tidy house, tidy mind goes the saying – so it follows that with an untidy house comes an untidy mind – all of which makes for a more messy and stressful way of living.

Indeed, if you are seeking true happiness, you really do need to do some serious decluttering.

It might seem a stretch to equate a more streamlined home with inner peace, but study after study has linked both physical and emotional decluttering with a greater sense of success and satisfaction with life.

It turns out that all the excess things we keep with us, both internally and externally, can have a profound impact on our current wellbeing – and our future emotional life.

Clutter in both our physical environment and relationships can keep us rooted in the past and block the flow of positive energy and forward momentum.

Just think about it for a moment. When we have too much junk and unwanted stuff in our lives, there simply isn't space for all those good things to enter – the more spiritually nourishing experiences that most of us thirst for. We all want more fulfilling relationships, greater success in our chosen field, clothes we love and a home we find beautiful, yet most of us crowd out the necessary spaces with an excess of mediocre, unused rubbish that adds little to our lives.

And while many of us view decluttering as simply the clearing out of our physical world, it is just as important that we sweep aside all the unnecessary mental and emotional debris from our interior world as well.

As you embark on your decluttering journey it is easy to become overwhelmed by the scale of the task or your seeming lack of progress without proper support and expert help to make the right changes in the right order. The easy-to-follow tips in this book will guide you through the decluttering process, step-by-step, so you won't feel daunted at the prospect.

Once you start to get rid of all that unnecessary physical and psychological baggage that is cluttering your days and disturbing your nights, your life will immediately change for the better.

So what are you waiting for? Read on for 100 ways to declutter your life – starting today…

# DECLUTTER YOUR MIND

While many of us view decluttering as simply the clearing out of our physical world, it is just as important that we sweep aside all the unnecessary mental and emotional debris from our interior world as well. It's an unfortunate part of the human condition to hold on to resentment, anger and disappointment, often for years after the initial act that caused these feelings.

Yet by refusing to let go of these negative emotions, it becomes difficult to allow gratitude in and feel full appreciation for the many good things in our life right now. The relationship between physical mess and emotional mess also supports a more holistic view of sorting out your life – you need to look at both before you can embark on a calmer, more organized existence.

# #1

## VISUALIZE HOW YOU WANT YOUR LIFE TO LOOK

--------------------------------

Spend the next few minutes thinking about your ideal life.
Would it involve a career change, meeting a life partner,
doing something positive for your family, or for society even?
By imagining your dream destination, you can start to think about
all the small steps it takes to get there.

Write down three things you'd love to happen in your life:

1 ...........................................................................................................

...........................................................................................................

...........................................................................................................

2 ...........................................................................................................

...........................................................................................................

...........................................................................................................

3 ...........................................................................................................

...........................................................................................................

...........................................................................................................

# #2
# UNCOVER WHAT'S HOLDING YOU BACK

--------------------------------

Note down all the situations or areas you think you need to address to help get you to where you would like to be. There are no wrong answers here. These are the things you believe are blocking or limiting you.

Is it the way your best never seemed to be good enough for one parent? Or has a partner made you feel undervalued while you were together? Drill into the details.

And be honest with yourself. This step is essential to declutter your emotions. For this you'll have to dig deep and uncover the old patterns you are still stuck in.

.........................................................................................

.........................................................................................

.........................................................................................

.........................................................................................

.........................................................................................

.........................................................................................

.........................................................................................

.........................................................................................

.........................................................................................

# #3
## QUIETEN THE MENTAL CHATTER

--------------------------------

At any given time of day our minds are cluttered with a constant background of chatter that is controlling how we think and feel. It keeps us from being present in the moment.

Staying in the moment can be really challenging, especially when our mind keeps on dragging us to places we don't want to go. For example, we might be trying to enjoying a sunny holiday abroad, but our mind keeps on chattering about the work we left behind. Or we are too busy wondering whether people will like our holiday photos on social media to actually enjoy the beautiful scenery.

Practising regular meditation is one of the best ways to train yourself to be wholeheartedly in the moment. But just like any other skill worth acquiring, mindfulness requires a lot of practice.

Downloading an app such as Calm or Headspace on to your smartphone is a great way to get started.

# #4
## BE MORE DECISIVE

---------------------------------

When you constantly put off making decisions, your brain becomes overwhelmed by all the clutter that's created by carrying all the variables of the decision-making process around with you. So, stop procrastinating and decide today. Whether it's about taking a new job, asking out someone you've fancied for ages or clearing out your kitchen cupboards – get it done. This doesn't mean making rash decisions – it's often still important to carefully evaluate all the pros and cons, but remember that we may never have all the information we need. So make up your mind, do what your heart tells you – and don't look back again.

# #5
## PRACTISE DEEP BREATHING

------------------------------

Take a deep breath. Pause. Exhale slowly. Repeat five times. How do you feel? Calmer, more in control? Deep breathing is a simple yet effective technique to clear your mind, induce tranquillity and elevate your mood instantly. It lowers the heart rate and blood pressure and stimulates the parasympathetic nervous system, which helps your body relax. As well as being a brilliant stress-reliever, breathing exercises also promote concentration and focus.

# #6
# DECLUTTER FRIENDSHIPS

----------------------------------

Do you have friends who are consistently taking more than they give, or who make you feel bad about yourself and never want to celebrate your achievements? Life's too short to put up with this sort of rubbish. Make a list of friends who aren't cutting the mustard and who you might be better off without. Ask yourself: how do these people really make you feel?

Are they adding to your life in any meaningful, supportive way? Or making you miserable or anxious?

Regardless of who they are or how long the history is, if people are a constant source of negativity in your life and add no value, then it's time to fade them out. Only by distancing yourself from these false friendships can you create space to let in more supportive and genuine people.

# #7
# LET GO
# OF ANGER

---

Many of us have a forgotten shelf somewhere that's crammed with too many pictures and knick-knacks to count, a messy spot that's a magnet for attracting dust and dirt in hard-to-reach areas. As a result, we can never face the thought of cleaning the shelf and so actively avoid it, letting the cobwebs build up over years.

Anger can work in the same way – with each rage-inducing event accumulating inside us over time, until the very idea of dealing with the source feels too overwhelming. But if built-up anger and resentment is getting in the way of your life, it's time to do something about it. A good place to start is to stop expecting people to be perfect – and taking their flaws and mistakes as a personal insult. If someone has an annoying habit that enrages you every time it happens (perhaps out of all proportion) then maybe let them off the hook – and yourself too. Try to let daily life happen without judgment and realize that most people are doing the best they can – just like you. This approach will help anger to dissipate and allow more compassionate feelings to grow instead.

# #8
# STOP HOLDING GRUDGES

--------------------------------

When something hurts us, evolutionary instinct encourages us to hang on to the pain to make sure we don't forget and can never be hurt in the same way again. But while that instinct remains useful for teaching children about danger, it's not a good way for fully grown adults to handle emotional relationships. Constantly looking backwards keeps you standing still – or crashing into obstacles on the path in front of you. Instead of holding on, let go of the need to punish and try to forgive and move past it. You can't change the past – only the way you respond to it. Forgive for your own sake at least, if not for the person who upset you in the first place.

# #9
# DON'T LET JEALOUSY RULE

-----------------------------------

Envious emotions can seriously clutter our hearts and minds if they're allowed free rein. In this era of social media oversharing it is a constant battle – we experience envy over other people's appearance, talents, relationships and lifestyles. Yet these feelings provide no positive contribution to our lives. So it's time to break free. Remind yourself that nobody has it all – comparing your life with others is always a losing proposition.

There will always appear to be people who have it better than you. At least on the surface. So if social media sucks you into an envy cycle then perhaps it is time to cut down your usage or even close your account. And remember, we always compare the worst of what we know about ourselves to the best assumptions we make about others. Be reminded, despite what Instagram might suggest, that nobody has the perfect life. Each person you meet in real life experiences problems, trials and weaknesses – just like you. This is what makes us human.

# #10
## LIVE WITH LESS FEAR

--------------------------------

Fear is another area of emotional clutter we often haul around with us unnecessarily. It's not possible to completely eliminate fear – and it's a useful instinct when it comes to sensing real danger. But the key is to not let any fear based on past experiences control you and stop you doing the things you want to do in life. This is particularly true when those fears are not rational. For example, just because you were made redundant in your last job, it doesn't mean it will happen again in your new role. Rationalize your fears and list all the logical reasons why the outcome you are most worried about is actually very unlikely to happen.

# #11
## TRAIN YOURSELF TO BE AN OPTIMIST

----------------------------------

Seeing life as a glass half-empty and always expecting the worst is one of the easiest but most damaging ways to fill our minds with emotional clutter that gets in the way of enjoying daily life. Think about how you bag up old clothes to give them to charity and try adopting the same approach to negative thinking – just give it all away. Don't hold on to such useless thoughts for another moment. Pessimists often end up missing enriching life experiences and pushing other people away; studies have even shown they don't live as long as optimists. So, make a conscious decision to hope for the best in all situations – and aim find a silver lining even when things do fall short of your expectations.

# #12
## KEEP TWO DIARIES

----------------------------------

Have one journal for writing down all the good stuff – jotting down all the nice things that happened and recording all the good feelings and your gratitude for them. Then keep another diary as an outlet for any negative crap. Think of it as a place to dump all the bad stuff – your anger, your frustrations, your fears and insecurities. Getting it all out on paper will lift a huge weight from you, enabling you to feel free and lighter.

But, and this is important, just as you wouldn't keep opening the lid of a rubbish bin to check what's inside, don't be tempted go back and read over your negative thoughts once you have offloaded them. This will only result in you reliving them and feeling bad again, which defeats the object of having ditched them in the first place! On the other hand, do get in the habit of regularly rereading your happiness journal, as going back over beautiful memories will boost your mood and encourage healthy feelings of thankfulness.

# PREPARING TO DECLUTTER YOUR HOME

Now you've done a bit of work decluttering your emotional life, you should be feeling more focused and in a better place to turn your attention to addressing the physical clutter in your life.

The remainder of this book will focus on physical spaces, but that doesn't mean it won't continue to contribute to your emotional wellbeing – as a raft of research has made a strong link between less clutter and lower stress levels. Indeed, all clutter starts between the ears, and our first task is to look at why we accumulate so much stuff – and why we find it so hard to throw away.

# WHY DO WE COLLECT CLUTTER?

--------------------------------

The fact that you're reading this book probably means you feel that clutter has in some way taken over your life. The first thing to understand is you are really not alone! At some point we've all felt overwhelmed by overflowing wardrobes, a kitchen crammed with so much useless stuff it's hard to cook, or a loft full to the brim with junk.

And yet, even when stuff is obviously serving no good purpose we have all experienced that strange sense of inertia that prevents us from just throwing it out. This reluctance is because as humans we are actually hardwired to hang on to stuff. Preserving resources is an evolutionary throwback to ensure we're not left empty-handed in times of scarcity.

But our life today is very different to that of our ancestors. We live in a time of plenty, when most people are more likely to have too much rather than too little – yet the habit of hoarding remains part of our brain circuitry.

Indeed, a recent study by Yale School of Medicine found that, for many, letting go is literally painful.

Researchers recruited both non-hoarders and hoarders, and then asked them to sort through items such as junk mail and old newspapers. Some of the items belonged to the scientists, but some actually belonged to the participants.

Participants had to decide what to keep and what to throw away. While all this was happening, their brain activity was tracked using an MRI scanner.

Unlike non-hoarders, hoarders showed increased activity in two specific areas of the brain when confronted with their own junk. These two areas – known as the "anterior cingulate cortex" and the "insula" – are both involved with psychological pain. The study found that the more a hoarder reported feeling "not right" about throwing something out, the stronger the activity in those pain parts of the brain.

Interestingly, these very same brain regions are responsible for producing overwhelming cravings in smokers or alcoholics who are trying to quit their habit. The stronger the addiction, the stronger the feelings of anxiety and discomfort, and the greater the urge to drink or smoke.

In habitual hoarders it appears that just the idea of throwing stuff away causes the brain to experience a similar distress signal. And as we're all programmed to avoid pain and discomfort, the brain will seek to relieve this anxiety, which means smokers light up a cigarette, drinkers pour a whisky and hoarders burrow away their junk.

Each time a hoarder hangs on to something, they seem to feel safer and calmer – and this sense of relief can become addictive.

We know that people with a tendency to hoard feel an irrational conviction that something seemingly old and useless could still have potential value one day in the future. The very idea that they might be throwing away something that could yet be of use becomes painful. And when it comes to something with some sentimental value attached to it, the urge to keep it forever is even stronger.

You don't have to be a hoarder to know what this attachment feels like – whether it's a favourite old jumper, a gift you've never used but can't bear to throw out, or every drawing your child ever did!

Knowing that there is a biological basis to our irrational impulse to accumulate clutter can be useful when it comes to overcoming the anxiety we associate with throwing stuff away.

And because we now know more about the science of addiction and how to rewire the brain, the good news is, whether you are an extreme hoarder or just an occasional stock-piler of junk, it is possible to change your habits. It's just a question of getting started.

# #13
# IDENTIFY YOUR DECLUTTER GOALS

----------------------------------

To stand any chance of successfully decluttering your life, you need to start breaking your streamlined dream life down into manageable milestones.

Trying to overhaul everything at once can make you feel overwhelmed before you've even begun. Indeed, the most crucial step to successfully completing any major life project is to first identify and then clearly define a series of smaller goals in a very clear and specific way.

# #14
## GET MOTIVATED

------------------------------

Getting fully motivated will help you to stay strong and stick to your plans when the temptation to fall back into old patterns and habits inevitably appears.

Start by making a list of compelling reasons why you want to stop hoarding. For example: "I want to be able to entertain guests in my home" or "I want to be able to relax more after a hard day at work."

1 .........................................................................................................................................
.........................................................................................................................................
.........................................................................................................................................
2 .........................................................................................................................................
.........................................................................................................................................
.........................................................................................................................................
3 .........................................................................................................................................
.........................................................................................................................................
.........................................................................................................................................

Review this list of motivations whenever you start to wobble in your course of action.

# #15

## USE VISUALIZATION TO HELP ACHIEVE YOUR GOAL

--------------------------------

One of the best life-coaching tools to help with goal setting is visualization. This popular technique simply means creating a vivid, mental image of a goal you would like to accomplish in the future.

   You set your mind to imagining a certain outcome in as much detail as possible. Asking yourself leading questions such as "what does it look like?" and "how do I feel when it is accomplished?" For instance, when it comes to decluttering your wardrobe, you might start by imagining rows of perfectly ordered shelves and colour-coded clothes rails. And you might also tap into the joy or pride and relief you might feel to be standing in front of them. Using these positive feelings as motivators to get you started is key.

# #16
## FIND A QUIET PLACE

--------------------------------

The first step in learning how to visualize is to find a quiet place
to clear your mind and imagine your goals.

You can choose your favourite spot in the house, a nice shady tree
in the garden, or anywhere that you know that you can sit peacefully
and not be disturbed. A quiet place is essential to having a good
visualization experience.

Once you have found the perfect spot, it's now time to relax and
clear your mind. When preparing for visualization, sit in a position
that will remain comfortable for a while. Close your eyes and relax
by taking a few deep, rhythmic breaths and clearing your mind of
all thoughts.

If you have trouble emptying your mind, continue to focus on your
breathing pattern, counting for five as you breathe in through the
nose and slowly down from 10 each time you breathe out. Repeat
this process until you are fully present in the moment and your mind is
empty. It can take a bit of practice, but stick with it.

# #17
# IMAGINE YOUR GOALS

----------------------------------

Now your mind is prepared, it's time to visualize those goals. In your mind's eye imagine all the details of the final day of your project. Think about what you are looking at and who else is present. Think about what it feels like, what you are wearing even. Visualize as many small details as you can.

A good way to kickstart visualization is to ask yourself what's known as the "Magic Wand Question". If you had magic wand, what would you transform – and what would the completed transformation look like? Don't worry about the practical reality or any obstacles to be overcome. Use this process as an opportunity to think about what will really make you feel happy and satisfied when it comes to decluttering your life. Have fun with it and dream big!

# #18
## GET IT ON PAPER
--------------------------------

While the future transformation is still fresh in your mind, write down below the six key ways your life will improve by learning to declutter and living a more minimalist lifestyle. Focus on the way you feel about yourself and your home. Be as specific as possible. The richer the details, the more meaningful and inspiring it will be.

1 .................................................................................................................
.................................................................................................................
2 .................................................................................................................
.................................................................................................................
3 .................................................................................................................
.................................................................................................................
4 .................................................................................................................
.................................................................................................................
5 .................................................................................................................
.................................................................................................................
6 .................................................................................................................
.................................................................................................................

# #19
## DON'T TRY AND DO IT ALL AT ONCE

--------------------------------

It's tempting to just go for it and try to blitz the whole house in one go. But not only will this impractical aim be exhausting and time consuming, a one-time blitz won't lead to lasting change when it comes to keeping clutter levels down in the future. The secret to any success is breaking it down into baby steps that are easy to achieve – and repeat. For example, if you have a large, expansive goal like "Clean the whole house" it may be hard to know when you're even actually finished. And it could take so long your motivation may fade and you'll be back at square one in terms of mindset. Instead, set a small, clear goal like "Clear the lounge bookshelf." With such a goal, it will be easy to know when you have completed it and the results will be very obvious – creating motivation and momentum for the next task. Alternatively, you can also set time-based goals, such as "I will work for one hour each day to clear clutter."

# #20
## GET A STRATEGY

------------------------------

To rid yourself of current clutter and keep future clutter at bay, you need to develop a clear strategy for organizing things. One of the most common problems is deciding the actual value of an item – and then where it should live. So decide on how you plan categorize the different items in your home, typically by item type or its common location – e.g. kitchen, living room, etc.

In each space that you clear, designate a few simple piles, such as items to donate, items to sell, stuff to trash, recycle or keep. Work on one area at a time until it's clear. Avoid just moving items from one area to another though, which brings us on to...

# #21
## GET A GOOD SYSTEM

--------------------------------

To make the process of decluttering simpler, you need an easy system to apply to every item of clutter. The best way to approach this is to sort items into one of three categories:

1) KEEPER: I'm definitely keeping this item
2) BIN IT: I'm definitely going to recycle or give away this item
3) UNDECIDED: I'm not sure

When it comes to number 1) the keep pile, set a simple rule that everything in it has to already have a place to go. A ready-made home for stuff you need and love.

The discard pile is also simple. You need to move it all out as soon as possible – bagging up stuff for the bin or charity shop, making sure to recycle as many items and materials as you can.

The unsure pile, however, will need further consideration. Get tough with your inner-hoarder and ask yourself the following:

Does it make me happy?
Have I ever used it?
Will I ever use it?

Unless an item has future use and continues to bring happiness, then it is probably a candidate for the discard pile. The aim is to quickly reduce your three piles to just two: Keepers and Bin It.

# #22

## HAVE A "BELONGS IN ANOTHER ROOM" BIN

---------------------------------

As well as having large bins or bags handy to put everything from your "bin it" pile into, plus one for the recycling centre and one for charity – you also need a "belongs in another room" keeper bin for the stuff that's staying but moving to another part of the house. Then you can transport stuff around from room to room easily and put it away as soon it is sorted.

# #23
# ONLY SORT ITEMS ONCE

---------------------------------

Avoid the tendency to put something to one side "until later" – as later rarely actually comes! Make your decision about each item you pick up straight away, ensuring you don't have to handle it again and again. If in doubt initially, use the undecided pile, but once you turn your full attention to sorting through that pile you need to again make snappy decisions.

The best way to control your inner procrastinator is to only allow yourself 30 seconds to look at an item before deciding how to categorize it. These decisions can be hard but they are not complicated – and your first instinct will usually be the right one. Plus, the longer you ponder over an item, the more memories it will spark, the greater your attachment will become and the harder it will be to get rid of it.

Once you've decided an item's fate, place it in the correct pile – and don't go back or give yourself any chance to change your mind about it later.

# #24

## DON'T BECOME DISTRACTED

--------------------------------

You may be tempted to try to multi-task while you're having a clear out – or even avoid the reality of what you're doing by preoccupying yourself with other activities. But this is a bad idea as you won't fully engage with the process of decluttering and overcome your fear of doing it in the process. There is a time to Instagram your life and this is not it!

So only focus on one task at a time and pick a time when you won't be disturbed.

# #25

## PICK A DECLUTTER SOUNDTRACK

--------------------------------

Having the TV on in the background or chatting on the phone is a no-no as it means you won't concentrate properly on the task in hand. However, playing some of your favourite songs is a good idea, as music can be very motivating and will make the task more fun.

# #26
## SET A TIME LIMIT

------------------------------

A full declutter is a marathon not a sprint – you need to preserve energy for the long haul. Setting and sticking to a limited time period can help keep you focused and ensure you don't become too overwhelmed with the amount you have to achieve. For example, decide to have a solid clearing-out of stuff for one hour – and then take a break. Have a snack, go for a 10-minute stroll or sit and meditate for a few moments. If you then find you have enough energy to go again, you could try a second hour.

# #27
## TRACK YOUR PROGRESS VISUALLY

------------------------------

As you slowly move through your home, room by room, keep track of the progress you've made and how you feel about it by taking pictures before and after your declutter. This can help you maintain momentum, and gain confidence to deal with the remainder of your home. Pictures are a great way to capture your achievements as you clear out each space.

# #28
# REDUCE SENTIMENTAL STUFF BY 75 PER CENT

--------------------------------

If you've always kept every childhood school report, every item of baby clothing, every love letter and holiday postcard, it's time to rationalize! Choose to save a few of the most special pieces and throw away the rest. You really don't need multiple versions of the same thing. If there is one particularly special item, such as a photo, then perhaps frame it and display it on the wall where it will bring even more joy.

The same approach can be used to cut down on children's artwork. Make it into a fun activity with your kids, ask them to choose a few favourite pieces with you and either display them or store them in a folder that will last.

And if you find throwing sentimental items away hard, why not photograph each item and save to a special "memories" folder on your laptop or in the iCloud first? You could even choose to display them on a digital photo frame. Then, not only are they stored safely – they will be seen more than ever before instead of hidden away.

# #29
## BOX IT UP FOR SIX MONTHS

------------------------------

If you simply cannot decide whether to keep an item or throw
it away, put it in a box for six months and store it somewhere
accessible in the cellar, garage or loft. At the same time, make a
clear a note on your calendar of when the six months is up.
Then, when that date comes around, commit to dealing with this
problem item immediately.

   The point of this exercise is that if you haven't opened the box
in all of that time, you can safely let it go without regret. This is a
great idea for people who hang on to items such as old magazines,
CDs, travel toiletries and other free samples – "just in case they
come in handy".

# #30
## JOURNAL YOUR WAY OUT OF CLUTTER AND CHAOS

--------------------------------

While a journal can't actually cut down decluttering for you, journalling your progress during and after your declutter can be an invaluable resource for changing your behaviour. As you let go of the past and embrace your new junk-free, more organized life, maintaining a journal of your journey will provide both motivation and momentum.

At first journalling may sound like being a teenager again and having homework, but the key is not to see the writing as a chore but as a tool for empowerment.

The simple act of regular progress reporting to yourself is one of the single best ways to break down your goals into manageable, bite-size chunks so the task in hand doesn't seem so overwhelming.

# #31
## GET HELP FROM A PROFESSIONAL

----------------------------------

These days there are a raft of professional declutterers available online and on local forums that can help you clear out your home if it's something you really can't face doing alone. Even if you only book them for a day to help you get started, having an objective person there with you while you're clearing out your belongings can help make the process easier. As well as lending a hand, a professional will give you suggestions and advice and will help you stay motivated to finish the job.

# #32
# AM I A HOARDER?

-----------------------------------

Sometimes collecting or living with clutter becomes the more serious problem of hoarding. But how can you tell the difference? One sign of a true hoarder is that you have huge amounts of items that serve no obvious purpose in your life – and seem useless or odd to others. These items aren't practical, they are not for decoration or to complete a collection. Instead it's the physical act of acquiring them and then hanging on to them that feeds the addictive impulse. Other key signs are having areas in your house you can't get to and clean or use for the purpose they are meant to. Finally, being over-sentimental about objects can also be a tell-tale sign.

We all have some personal items we keep from the past that we feel very strongly about, but the emotions that hoarders feel about objects are different – they overvalue everything – not just the odd special item – and as a result become far too emotionally invested in their stuff and can't bear to let any piece of it go.

If you tick one or more of the criteria above, then launching into a full-scale clean-up of your home all at once is likely to be too emotionally distressing. You probably need to get to the root of your problem with hoarding first – and that usually means getting some professional help.

Experts recommend asking your doctor to refer you for cognitive behavioural therapy (CBT) with a trained therapist. This talking therapy can help you understand the reasons why you hoard – and more importantly, how to improve the decision-making, organization and problem-solving skills you need to overcome it.

Visit: www.helpforhoarders.co.uk or hoardinguk.org for more help and advice.

# LIVING ROOM

The living room is one of the hardest rooms in your home to keep neat on a daily basis. That's because while it generally gets a lot of use, your average lounge doesn't contain a huge amount in the way of storage options. You may have some bookcases and a TV cabinet, but they don't hide much, which means remotes and blankets are often left hanging around. Keeping your living room surfaces clear is essential for an inviting space, so clutter-containment is key. Think of what you really do in that space and keep only things that you will frequently use there. And remember, even if you technically have room for something, it doesn't mean that you should automatically keep it! Learning to relax with less is about stripping back to only the essentials we *really* need.

# #33
## GET STORAGE SAVVY

--------------------------------

If you don't have them, create permanent storage spaces for commonly used items such as books and internet routers. Floating shelving is ideal. Invest in a set of stylish storage baskets – they're great for holding extra blankets, storing magazines, or tidying up kids' toys. Decorative boxes are great for storing necessities such as remotes, while a pretty tray works well on a coffee table to both display your favourite objects and make moving them out of the way easier.

# #34
## CLEAR OUT YOUR CUPBOARDS

--------------------------------

Once you have done the surface decluttering, it is time to dig a little deeper. Start with bookcases, cupboards and side tables. Empty them, assess the items they store and then return them to their proper storage spaces. Have a bag handy for any rubbish. Put books away, action any post and return remote controls to their proper places. Then go through drawers looking for any items that you don't love and need – be prepared to find lots of random objects that have been tucked out of sight a long time ago!

# #35
## DITCH THOSE DISCS

------------------------------------

Increasingly we live in an age of streaming media – from music to movies. So take a long look at any shelves or cupboards full of CDs or DVDs. This may include some old favourites that you are proud to display, but ask yourself: is a disc even how you play them anymore? With technology continuing to move towards cloud storage and streaming, you can save lots of valuable storage by decluttering all your old media.

# #36
## MOVE ON TO ELECTRONICS

------------------------------------

Remove everything that is not connected to your current television or music system. Are you using it? Does it work? Even as we upgrade our entertainment equipment it's amazing that we still hang on to old cables, chargers and remote controls. Store the add-on items you do need, such as computer gaming controls, in the cupboard closest to your screen.

# #37
## QUESTION THAT MAGAZINE RACK

------------------------------

These are secret clutter collectors! Although they signal good intentions of being tidy, when you take a closer look they are always full of out-of-date magazines, old post and other junk. Do you really need one? If not – ditch or donate it! And perhaps rationalize your regular reading material also – if a new issue of a magazine arrives and you have still not read the last one perhaps it is time to unsubscribe.

# #38
# EXERCISE EQUIPMENT

----------------------------------

You might think sticking an exercise bike in front of the TV is a great idea to get you working out, but unless you're actually going to use it regularly, it just ends up being an eyesore or a place to dry clothes! While it is vital to look after your health, a treadmill, rowing machine or cross trainer-shouldn't be in the living room if at all possible. Is there an area in a spare room, garage or garden room that it could be moved to instead?

# #39
## CUSHION CULL

----------------------------------

We get it – there are some gorgeous colourful cushions out there, and the magpie in you yearns to gather up all these pretty things and take them home. But too many cushions all over your living room can quickly become clutter – not to mention impractical. As a rule of thumb, if you need to move them all before you can actually sit down, you have too many! Try halving the amount.

# #40
## PAPERWORK PILE PURGE

----------------------------------

The living room should be a place to put your feet up, so piles of paperwork just remind us of all the unfinished stuff we still have to do. Instead, create a holding section in your kitchen or hall for all incoming paperwork and set a weekly time to action it. Avoid touching it until you're actually ready to deal with it – that way you won't keep moving it around the house until it is impossible to find!

# #41
## WASHING OR IRONING

------------------------------

Much like paperwork, having piles of laundry stacked everywhere is simply a reminder of all that is left to be done. Unless you're actually about to iron, the living room is not the place for piles of ironing to live. Ditto the ironing board and iron themselves.

# #42
## TACKLE THOSE TOYS

------------------------------

Every parent has stepped on bits of plastic before. And hearing battery-powered toys suddenly chirp or burst into song of an evening is not relaxing! First of all, make sure your children have sufficient toy storage in their bedroom. Realistically, some toys may need to be stored in the living room but this doesn't mean they have to be visible once the kids are in bed. Buy an attractive toy chest or easy pull-out baskets for existing cupboards, and then go through and assess every toy for wear and tear, asking:

Does it still work?
Do the kids still play with it?

Then either bin, donate or store away each toy.

# #43
## KEEP UP THE GOOD WORK

--------------------------------

Declutter your lounge regularly to keep on top of things. For young children, incorporate "tidy-up time" into their evening routine – make playing with toys contingent on them later putting the same toys away in designated boxes.

# #44
## DOWNSIZE NEXT TIME YOU BUY

--------------------------------

Think carefully next time you buy furniture. Too much will make even tidy living rooms look cluttered. In the UK, we commonly choose large, bulky, furniture – particularly dining tables and sofas. If we can afford the space then this isn't a problem, but according to IKEA, Britons have the smallest homes in Europe – which means many of us don't! Think about buying smaller, more streamlined furniture, tables which can fold away or fold out to become bigger. Also, "double-duty" furniture with storage incorporated such as ottoman coffee tables or footstools that can have items like blankets stored inside them, are great. And do you really need that four-seater sofa – or will a smaller one look nicer and save on space?

# DECLUTTER YOUR KITCHEN

For many of us the kitchen has become the heart of the home – a centre not just for cooking but for eating and entertaining too. This new style of open-plan living and socializing brings many advantages, but it does make keeping your kitchen clutter-free a bigger challenge. This single space will have many different types of items stored within it, not least because – unlike the living room, which tends to be lacking in drawers and shelves – the kitchen is nothing but storage. This makes it a powerful magnet for unused gadgets, gizmos and junk – so let's get sorting!

# #45

## CONCENTRATE ON YOUR COUNTERTOPS

--------------------------------

Move as many items as possible off the countertops and into storage spaces. Keep only what you use every single day on the surfaces. This will leave you more room to actually prepare food, which will encourage you to cook more often!

# #46
## GET INTO THOSE CUPBOARDS

---

The first step is to completely empty each space, assessing every item, and then put everything back where it belongs. Start with your biggest storage spaces first, such as the pantry and upper cabinets. Then move on to the lower cabinets, drawers and the space under the kitchen sink.

Your kitchen cupboards might be full of mismatched china, unused utensils and even that cheese fondue set you were gifted, to name just a few of the common items we hang on to. Get rid of anything that's damaged, neglected or unpleasant to use. Again, less is more. You need trusted, quality kitchen tools that are fun to use and easy to find!

When it comes to foodstuffs, ditch anything past its sell-by-date, unwanted gifts or foods you know you will never eat. Donate anything reusable – bin the rest, putting actual food in food waste whenever you can.

# #47
## BE RUTHLESS

--------------------------------

It may be tempting to hang on to objects in case you need them "someday", but that's not a valid reason to hoard stained, mismatched Tupperware or a cracked serving bowl. For every 20 things you give up, there's a small chance you may end up regretting one. Save the space for something you're using now. Donate storage containers without matching lids, dishes you no longer use, and cookie cutters collecting dust to free up valuable room in your cupboards.

Get rid of any sets of crockery where you don't have at least four place settings. Do the same with mismatched cups and mugs or anything chipped.

Then take a long hard look at those kitchen gadgets and appliances – the ones that sounded so amazing, but you've barely or never used. Donate or sell any of these space-sucking items – we all know secretly that "someday" will never come!

# #48
## CONSIDER EASY ACCESS

----------------------------------

Once you've pared down these items, streamline your kitchen to enhance the experience of making and eating a meal. Creating "zones" by grouping similar items together allows you to see everything you own and makes finding your cooking essentials a breeze. And think about use frequency. Anything you use on an almost daily basis should be easily accessible, obviously. Store medium-frequency use items such as cake tins and extra-large saucepans on mid-height shelves or cupboards. While rarely used appliances such as pasta machines and ice cream makers – but only if you actually use them – can go in those hardest-to-reach top cabinets. Otherwise they should be donated.

# #49
# THINK VERTICALLY

--------------------------------

Do you just stack saucepans and baking trays in any old jumble? Try applying some logic and order instead. Install stationery file dividers into deep drawers and you can have a nifty way to line items such as trays, baking sheets and lids up vertically. IKEA make good file dividers. And always stack your mixing bowls, pots and pans and china – in size order. When storing your best china, place a sheet of kitchen towel between each piece to help prevent any chips or breakage caused by friction.

Install some pullout drawers to maximize space in pantries and lower cabinets. You can also add free-standing corner shelves to existing cupboards to make sure no space is wasted.

# #50
## MAKE OVER YOUR FOOD PANTRY

--------------------------------

One of the quickest and simplest ways to make your pantry look neat and tidy is to transfer food items into matching jars. Items such as flour, cereal, seeds, nuts, rice, pasta and dried fruits look Instagram-ready displayed in glass Kilner jars. Group foodstuffs together and label the jars in large print so you know at a glance what they contain. Keep all your spices on one shelf, and then all your baking items on another.

# #51
# FRESHEN UP YOUR FRIDGE

------------------------------

Start by removing everything from your fridge and cleaning inside thoroughly with a sponge and hot soapy water. Pull out drawers and wash thoroughly in the sink.

Then throw away all open food, all condiments past their use-by-date or unused because you didn't like them. Again, put actual food into a food waste bin for collection by your local authority if they provide this service.

Now it's time to put things back. If your refrigerator shelves are adjustable, take a moment to plan what you want to go where and place them accordingly. As you replace each item, be sure it's clean.

# #52

## STREAMLINE YOUR FREEZER

----------------------------------

Consider a full defrost to clean it thoroughly and start again. Too much build up of ice and frost creates clutter on its own. As for food, get ruthless and remove anything that's over three months old or that you know you don't actually like. Despite your good intentions at the time, if you have frozen leftovers that you have not touched in a month you are unlikely to use them ever. Repeat this clear-out once a fortnight to keep your freezer clean and clutter free with limited effort.

# #53

## PUT NON-KITCHEN STUFF AWAY

----------------------------------

Lastly, you're not finished in this room until you've returned everything that belongs elsewhere in the house to its proper storage space. Just because the kitchen has lots of drawers doesn't mean they need to be filled with non-kitchen junk! If you are determined to keep it but it doesn't belong with food and cooking stuff, move it to another room now.

# DECLUTTER
# YOUR
# BEDROOM

To be properly restful your bedroom should be an oasis of calm – not a scene of constant chaos. This means the number of possessions stored there should be low. Yet it's all too common for bedrooms to become a general dumping ground for laundry, unpacked bags, beauty products, books and other random items. And because it's generally not a place visitors see, it's often the last room you get around to clearing. But in truth, decluttering the place where you sleep every night should be one of your top priorities. Since an unmade bed can make the whole room feel messy, get in the habit of making it every morning for a bit of instant order. After the bed is made, glance around as if you are a visitor and this is your first time in the space. Notice the first things that stand out, then think about what needs to change – what can stay and what *really* needs to go?

# #54

## TACKLE YOUR BEDSIDE TABLES

---------------------------------

This is a spot where all sorts of junk typically accumulates. Remove anything from the surface that shouldn't be there and put it in your "belongs elsewhere" bin. This may include books you've already finished reading, used paper, post you need to answer and cups you need to wash. Throw out or recycle anything that you no longer use, such as empty tissue boxes, pens that have gone dry, or phone chargers that no longer work.

Do the same with the tops of your chests of drawers and blanket boxes. Pay attention to any clothing that is strewn about. Anything that needs folding or hanging goes into the "put away" pile.

# #55
## DRESSING TABLE DRESS-DOWN

--------------------------------

Sort out all that beauty clutter. Be ruthless, only keeping items you've used in the last week or so on the top. Things you have used recently but don't need daily can go into drawers. Resist the urge to just shove things back into drawers without careful consideration, however; instead bin or recycle any rubbish or items you haven't used in more than six months.

   Spend some time putting earrings into pairs, untangling twisted items – and binning anything broken or missing its twin. If you don't already have one, invest in a decent jewellery box that's big enough to fit your whole collection. Choose a multi-layered box and make sure it has separate pull-out sections for earrings, necklaces, bracelets and rings. If you can see all of your collection just by opening up the box, you won't need to get everything out each time you're looking for the item you want to wear. Now get into the habit of putting any items worn that day back in their spot each night.

# #56
## BE RUTHLESS WITH ORNAMENTS

--------------------------------

If you've been hanging on to old presents, family "treasures" or other ugly trinkets solely out of guilt – now is the time to stop. If you don't love them and they don't make you smile, give them away. Your goal is to make your home clutter-free and comfortable for you. Remember, your affection and love for the person who gave you these objects doesn't change just because you let go of their gifts.

# #57
## DEVELOP A "DEAL WITH IT NOW" HABIT

--------------------------------

Make a promise to yourself to put your clothes away immediately, whether it's clean laundry or your office outfit at the end of a work day. By taking the time to put your things where they belong, you'll keep the space tidy and keep your clothes looking good for longer. You'll also be less likely to buy new items just because you can't find what you need. Likewise, as soon as you've read a book or magazine, shelve it, recycle it, give it to a friend or donate it to charity. This will ensure that the pile by the side of your bed doesn't start getting too big again.

# #58

## TACKLE THAT WARDROBE

--------------------------------

A proper clothing cull requires a slightly different approach to decluttering elsewhere. Probably the easiest way to approach this sort-out is to work by type. That means starting with shoes, then boots, then dresses, then denim, etc.

It's much easier to decide to toss or keep a pair of jeans if you're looking at your entire jean collection all at once. So start pulling out different types of clothing and decide what you'll toss and keep.

Try them on in front of a mirror right now – and ask yourself honestly:

Does this look nice?
Does it fit well?
Do I feel good wearing it?
Can I see myself wearing it again soon?

If you answer yes to all these questions, it stays – if you get a no though, it's bye-bye time!

Anything that is too big or too small, worn out or full of holes or badly stained has no place in your wardrobe. Decluttering professionals say you should really aim to minimize your clothes to 20 to 30 items. This carefully curated capsule wardrobe should contain all your everyday essentials, plus a few special outfits.

# #59
# FOUR IS THE FLOOR FOR SHOES

----------------------------------

If you drill down to absolute basics you really only need four pairs of shoes: smart heels, smart flats, casual lace-ups and boots. Get into the mindset that everything else is extra. Of course, you'll probably keep more pairs than that, but make sure each extra set really earn their space. This could be because they offer a practical alternative (for example, trainers if you like running) or just a pair you are truly passionate about. Anything that brings real happiness you should keep of course.

# #60
## CREATE A HOLIDAY BOX

--------------------------------

Realistically, there aren't many days a year when it's sunny enough in the UK to wear strappy dresses, kaftans and sandals, so having them permanently clog up a sizeable portion of your wardrobe just doesn't make sense. Get a box just for true summer gear and store it up high out of season.

As with holiday clothes, special occasion garments can be stored away from your everyday wardrobe – after all, a ball gown or wedding hat takes up a significant amount of room, and probably only gets worn once a year at most. Pack them away carefully using acid-free tissue paper to keep them in perfect condition. And make sure the box is clearly labelled so you know exactly what's in there, before putting it away on a high-up shelf or above a wardrobe.

# #61
## PROTECT YOUR CLOTHES

-----------------------------------

One of the joys of creating a clutter-free wardrobe is that you can actually take care of and protect your clothes properly. Once you've done your clear-out, first clean the entire inside of the wardrobe or chest of drawers, ideally using natural cleaning products. Next, add in some form of moth protection – hanging sachets are a good option for wardrobes, and can be bought easily online. Avoid wire hangers as they can ruin the shape of clothes. Opt instead for skinny, wooden hangers which don't take up too much room.

# #62

## STOP SEEING WARDROBES AS HIDING PLACES

--------------------------------

You don't put clothes in a wardrobe just to get them out of sight. You need to think of your wardrobe as an organizing tool. At a minimum, this means hanging clothes by type – for example trousers, skirts, jackets, dresses. To go one step further, order the colours from light to dark. Another expert tip is to turn all the hangers the wrong way around, so the hooks face you. Then, the first time you wear each item you can turn the hook the right way. After six months, any items not turned the right way have never been worn, which makes them the prime candidates to take to the charity shop.

# #63
## MAXIMIZE YOUR HANGING SPACE

------------------------------

Install some double rails in your wardrobe – with the lower one hanging about halfway down, so it's perfect for hanging shirts, skirts and other shorter items. You don't even need to install them – just look for the type that hooks on to your existing rail. Shelf dividers will prevent piles of sweaters from collapsing and are great for organizing handbags and scarves.

Finally, a good shoe system will help keep everything off the floor, whether you prefer clear shoe boxes, an over-the-door rack, or traditional wardrobe floor shoe racks.

# #64
# DO A SEASONAL DETOX

-----------------------------------

As the seasons change, so do your wardrobe needs. At the start of every new season take a few moments to review this season's capsule wardrobe. Eliminate anything that no longer fits, or perhaps just feels like last year's style, and move any out-of-season garments to the harder-to-reach areas.

# #65
## CREATE YOUR DREAM LINEN CUPBOARD

------------------------------

A perfectly ordered linen cupboard, filled with neat shelves of towels and bedding, is a thing of beauty. To get yours in order – and keep it that way – place everyday towels, sheets, and other linens at the front and centre so you don't have to disturb everything when you need to get them out. And store infrequently used items such as beach towels, holiday tablecloths and out-of-season blankets on harder-to-reach upper shelves.

A great way to avoid sorting through individual bed sheets every time you need a new set, is to store sets in bundles. Make a bundle by folding the under sheet and duvet cover and all but one pillowcase together, and then tucking all these folded items inside the remaining pillowcase to make a tidy pack. Simple!

# BATHROOM

While the bathroom might not be the most obvious room to amass clutter, its many drawers and cabinets can house all manner of half-forgotten products. There's the treatments tried once and then set aside, the bottles with just a squeeze of shampoo left, various pills from past illnesses – and much more besides. In fact, women alone use an average of 12 beauty products per day, from shampoo to mascara, according to figures from the US Environmental Working Group.

Twelve may sound like a lot – but how many do you actually have stored in your bathroom cabinets? Fifty? Sixty? More? If you're a habitual hoarder of beauty buys then it's time for a product amnesty to clear out all that clutter – because living the simple life really is more beautiful in the long run.

# #66

## START WITH YOUR BATHROOM CABINETS

---------------------------------

Take everything out and discard outdated medications, kid's bath toys that have gone black and mouldy, makeup and skincare products that are past their best – plus anything you haven't used at all in the last year. Recycle any plastic you can. Unused prescription medication can be properly disposed of at a pharmacy. Unopened toiletries can often be donated to a charity or a women's shelter.

Sort the rest into piles and give the cabinet a good clean.

Then put everything you're definitely keeping – apart from any medicines, which we'll come to next – immediately back into the cabinet, storing the items you use the most often, such as toothbrushes, contact lens solution and face wash, at eye level.

Only store a few rolls of toilet paper in the bathroom itself – the rest can live in the linen cupboard or cellar to save on space.

# #67
## KEEP MEDICINES SAFE

--------------------------------

Although we commonly store them in the bathroom, it's actually a much better idea to move medications and first-aid items elsewhere, as they aren't suited to the steamy atmosphere of a bathroom and can spoil and become damp quickly. You're better off keeping medicines in a linen cupboard, kitchen cupboard or other cool, dry place.

Organize all the items into separate open holding boxes, grouping them by illness, for example: cold and flu, tummy troubles, pain relief, hay fever etc. Then store on a high cupboard shelf, well out of reach of children and pets.

# #68
## CLEAR THE LEDGES AND EDGES

--------------------------------

Follow the same clear and clean routine around the bath and shower, only allowing one or two everyday use items to return there. All the others must be binned or given away if not used – or put into cabinets or drawers if they're used but less frequently.

Use a glass mason jar or similar to contain both your toothbrush and multiple makeup brushes to help neaten up the area around your sink.

Add hooks to the back of doors or on walls to keep in-use towels hung tidily, and have a basket under the sink to store clean towels.

# #69
## KEEP IT UP

------------------------------

Be strict about what you bring back in going forward. Stop bulk buying products or getting tricked by BOGOF deals. And don't take the mini toiletries from hotels or accept cosmetic samples from department stores unless you know you will definitely use them. The reality is, most of us never get around to using these items and they just end up taking up needless space in our cupboards and drawers.

# DECLUTTER YOUR HALLWAY

Your home's main entrance is obviously one of the highest traffic areas, and even small hallways can quickly turn into a dumping ground for discarded shoes, junk mail – and goodness knows what else if you let it. But remember, it's the first area other people see when entering your house and can therefore set the tone for the rest of the property. Just as important, it's the first area you see every time you come home and can therefore have a disproportionate effect on your own mood, so it's critical your hallway always looks clutter free and calm.

# #70
## CLEAR THE CONSOLE TABLE

--------------------------------

A hallway table is the place where everything gets discarded and dumped upon entering the house – indeed it gets cluttered so quickly it usually needs a daily purge. To get started, go through all the items on the top, making a quick decision on whether to bin or keep each one. Then go through each drawer, removing the contents and doing the same. The hall tends to pick up a lot of clutter from other rooms, so spend some time putting away things from elsewhere that have made their way there.

# #71
## CREATE A DROP SPOT FOR DAILY ESSENTIALS

---

Having a dedicated space for your keys, sunglasses or handbag will save you from searching for misplaced items every morning. Use a stylish tray or small wooden box to store these important items in – this reliable resting place will make your mornings easier while still keeping the hall table looking tidy.

# #72

## SORT JACKETS AND SHOES

--------------------------------

Do you really need all those jackets or shoe options by the door?
If your winter coat is still hanging up in summer or your flip-flops are
still around in autumn, then it's time to put them away. Only your most
frequently used coats and shoes should be on display in the hall.
If you don't already have a better place to store spare coats and
shoes, then think about adding a dedicated cupboard.
Speaking of which…

# #73
# TAMING CUPBOARD CHAOS

-------------------------------

If you do have a hall coat cupboard then it needs regular decluttering just like any other wardrobe. Just because it's hidden away doesn't mean it needs to hoard unseasonal styles. Start with shoes and boots, then jackets, followed by accessories. Keep, donate or bin any items you don't love or need.

# #74
## THINK ABOUT GETTING A SHOE CUPBOARD

--------------------------------

Having somewhere to put away shoes is one of the single biggest ways to make a difference to the feel of your hallway. Having no footwear left out immediately makes the space feel tidier and more welcoming. You can buy great, simple shoe cupboards, or if you can't find one the right size for your space, think about getting a local carpenter to create a bespoke one. It shouldn't cost too much, provided you shop around and get a couple of different quotes.

# #75
# HAVE A PLAN TO KEEP CLUTTER AWAY

--------------------------------

To ensure your hall stays clutter free, sort your post as soon as it arrives before putting it down. That means immediately opening anything that could be important and recycling any junk mail. Make decluttering a regular thing. No matter how small your hall, the best way to keep it organized is to have a declutter once a week. Try setting a time – such as every Sunday morning – to blitz it for 10 minutes.

# CHILDREN'S ROOMS

If there's one room you wish you could lock the door on and never look at again, it's probably your child's room! Thanks to the endless piles of toys, books, clothes and crafts in rotation at any one time, keeping this area clutter-free can feel like an impossible and endless task. Here are some tricks that can help make the transformation – and maintenance – easier.

# #76
## INVOLVE KIDS FROM THE START

----------------------------------

Although your first instinct might be to wait until your children are at nursery or school so you can chuck stuff away without complaint, getting your kids to help with a declutter is actually a really good idea. You might think they'll find it boring, but in reality most find it fun and will want to have a say in how their toys are organized. Involving them at the outset will also help ensure they feel some ownership over the project, so they'll be more inclined to keep things tidier — or at the very least, they'll know where everything should be stored!

It's not worth asking kids to choose what should stay or go – they will inevitably refuse to part with even the smallest item of tat. Instead, ask them to show you around their room – pointing out to you their favourite bits and why. This will give you a good sense of which things are most important to them – and what could perhaps now be safely donated to younger children via family or a charity shop.

# #77
## EXPLAIN HOW ALL STUFF HAS A HOME

------------------------------

Do you remember your parents telling you to "put all that junk away" as a child when your room was messy? This is actually a pretty negative way of expressing a wish for tidiness, but with a simple language tweak you can easily reframe this task in a more positive light. Younger children have a natural affinity for personalizing toys and other objects, so saying things such as "Where do we want this to live?" or "Shall we find this toy a nice home?" makes sense to them and better capture their imagination, making them keener to help.

# #78
## GIVE THEM PERMISSION TO DITCH STUFF THEY DON'T WANT

--------------------------------

Too much stuff can actually be overwhelming for kids, but they also don't know how to say no or give up things they no longer need. Give them the chance to sort out a pile of toys they no longer play with "to help some children who don't have many toys". The idea that their toys are getting a new home feels much more positive and like doing something good – rather than just getting rid of stuff for the sake of it.

# #79
## MAKE IT A GAME

--------------------------------

If possible, try making clearing up feel like play. Ask your child to collect six items to put back in their "homes" at the end of the day – and time them as they do it, with a prize for taking less than two minutes, for example. This feels more manageable than just "tidy everything up" and can help reinforce the habit of daily tidies.

# #80
# BE A NEAT FREAK

------------------------------------

Kids mirror what their parents are doing and even something as small as putting away your shoes, jacket and keys every time you get home acts as a lesson in action. Tidy parents equal tidy kids – so lead by example!

# #81
# GET IT OFF THE FLOOR AND SURFACES

--------------------------------

Clear out the desk drawers by neatly framing some of your child's best art masterpieces and hanging them in their bedroom.

Store toys and stuffed animals in their own baskets, but remember: the deeper the storage container, the harder it is to find something and the easier it is for the mess to start up again, so don't buy huge ones.

Instead of storing books on traditional bookcases, stand them upright in a shallow bin or storage basket. A child can easily flip through and pull out her favourites, but more importantly, it's a lot easier for little fingers to replace books in a bin than back on a shelf.

Another way to clear floor space is by hanging baskets from the ceiling to be filled with anything that needs a home.

Box things up under the bed: Spare bedding, out-of-season clothes and old toys they won't let go of just yet can live under the bed. You can buy canvas or wooden boxes to fit under most bed heights to help utilize every bit of space available.

Run shelving around the room: If you've used up all the cupboard, box and chest space in the room, then try adding a discreet shelf around it. This space is perfect for storing cuddly toys when kids are young and photo frames as they get older.

Just because your child's room has an awkward corner or sloped eaves doesn't mean the edges are out of bounds. Fixing a made-to-measure cupboard into these areas can create more room to store items your little hoarder can't bear to part with.

# #82

## HAVE A KIDS' "BELONGS IN ANOTHER ROOM" BIN

---

Kids leave stuff all over the house, and getting this under control can be a full-time job. Create a "belongs in another room" bin specifically for your kids to use and remind them that they're not finished tidying until they've returned everything that belongs elsewhere around the house to its proper place straight away. Don't let them leave anything lingering in the bin!

# #83

## DESIGNATE MINI CLEAN-UP TIMES

---

It's always easier to get the kids onboard to help if there are only a few items they need to put away.

Children like to do fun things fast, so do it regularly rather than leaving it until it looks like a bomb went off in their playroom, leaving both you and your kids feeling overwhelmed. A ten-minute tidy-up time after dinner each night is a manageable amount of time and, by doing a little and often, you should avoid needing to spend another whole day blitzing the area.

# CELLAR
# & LOFT

Both the loft and cellar spaces are prone to becoming a dumping ground for all those things that you're not ready to get rid of, yet don't really love or need. Whether you dream of turning your loft or basement into a more usable home space – or you're just tired of being faced with an overwhelming mess every time you enter – it's time to get them sorted once and for all.

The problem is, these storage spaces are both so out-of-sight, out-of-mind that it's all too easy to forget about all the stuff that lives there, adding more and more to it as time passes – and never really thinking about what's actually there. This means that when you finally need to declutter properly, perhaps as part of a house move, you might have rather a large task on your hands. But fear not, there are some simple stress-free ways to get started and shift that mess.

# #84

## BE HONEST – CAN YOU REALLY SELL IT?

--------------------------------

Many of us keep heaps of stuff in the cellar or loft that we have a vague plan for selling. But years later we still have a pile of boxes and no cash!  Again, be sensible when hanging on to items – think about how much time you will need to put into selling versus your return. Flog any high-ticket items and donate the rest to charity – you'll feel so much better for letting it go!

# #85
## SHOULD IT STAY OR GO?

------------------------------

Do an inventory and make of list of what stuff is reasonable to keep and what needs to be ditched.

Allowed to stay:

- Household supplies, bulk-buy toilet paper, laundry liquid and other similar items.

- Half-full paint cans – but only keep colours that are actually on your wall, so you have them handy for touch-up purposes.

- Extra dining chairs, used when guests come, and leaves to extend tables.

- DIY toolboxes and items like lightbulbs that you don't use often but might need to grab quickly.

Time to say goodbye:

- Ditch anything broken or unwanted, and also remember that most cellars are damp and so not the right place for anything that can warp, mould or mildew, for example letters, magazines, photos and cardboard boxes, plus mattresses, pillows and cushions.

# #86
## DESIGNATE DIFFERENT ZONES

--------------------------------

Now it's time to create a storage plan. Think of all the things you found in your cellar during the decluttering phase and create some distinct zones – perhaps according to activity or season.

This will help keep the clutter and chaos under control and make it easier to find stored things when you need them. Make large, clear labels for each area and start piling items up by each label.

# #87
# INSTALL SOME SHELVING

--------------------------------

If at all possible, never store anything directly in contact with the cellar floor where damp can creep in. It's a good idea to get some sturdy shelving in place, which will allow air to circulate while also enabling you to see exactly what you have stored.

# #88
## ELIMINATE TOOLBOXES WITH A WALL STORAGE SYSTEM

-----------------------------------

Plastic containers and shelves are ideal for items you're looking to store in the cellar, but what about items you use more regularly? If you keep your DIY tools in your cellar, having easy access to them needs to be high on the priority list.

One way to achieve this is to create a system for hanging them on a wall. This can be done easily by using various hook sizes, or getting a pegboard – have a look on Pinterest for ideas and then pop into your local DIY store for supplies.

# #89

## UPGRADE YOUR LAUNDRY AREA

--------------------------------

If you have your washing machine and tumble dryer in the cellar, there are lots of things you'll want to store to go along with them – such as detergent and clothes baskets. Installing a cupboard – free-standing or fixed – can help organize messy laundry items, so they're out of sight but easily accessed. This in turn will improve the look and functionality of your space.

# #90

## DO A YEARLY INVENTORY

--------------------------------

Now that you've gone through a lot of effort to sort your cellar, make sure it stays that way. Once a year, review exactly what's in there and get rid of items that are no longer needed. Kick the habit of continually adding new items without sorting through the things you already have.

# GARDEN

Just as happens inside the house, pretty much every horizontal surface in your garden – be it tables, decking or even the garden path – can end up becoming a magnet for all those items that never quite made it back into the house, garage or potting shed. And unfortunately, these things have a way of becoming "invisible" to us.

Whether it's a bicycle lying on the lawn, an abandoned hose or a broken child's swing, outdoor spaces can just as easily become cluttered with life's debris as our indoor spaces. One of the quickest ways to improve the appearance of any garden is to spend a weekend decluttering it. By doing so you'll be creating space to give the items you love – and your beautiful plants and flowers – room to breathe, and maintaining an outdoor oasis for you and your loved ones to enjoy.

# #91

## MAKE IT PRETTY WITH SOME QUICK WINS

--------------------------------

In the spring and summer months, it's easy to make your garden look its best by just adding a few hanging baskets and pots of colourful plants. You don't need to be a good gardener to put a few things in pots and the difference it makes to your space can be dramatic. If you have more money to spend and your furniture is beyond repair, invest in some new garden furniture. Alternatively, upcycle, mend and treat the furniture you already have as an autumn and winter outside will cause wear and tear.

# #92
## SORT YOUR SHED

-----------------------------------

Just like cellars and loft spaces, sheds are notorious clutter magnets – much of which is likely to be rubbish. So be prepared to get your hands dirty, brush away some interesting cobwebs and make several trips to your local recycling centre or tip.

Organize everything you decide to keep in your shed in wooden storage boxes, labelling them just as you would in indoor storage spaces. Most home stores and garden centres offer good shed storage systems to help you stay organized, but very regularly used items are better kept out loose for ease of use.

Sort through all the garden tools and repair or recycle broken ones. Keep usable tools in good shape by cleaning them. Then put them away neatly.

Try eBay or local recycling websites to find a new home for items that are still useful but that you no longer want.

# #93
## DON'T FORGET THE GARAGE!

--------------------------------

Be honest, can you actually get your car into yours?! If not, you're far from alone with one in four of us unable to squeeze our motor into its rightful home thanks to too much clutter, according to American research.

Even if you don't have a car or are happy using your garage as an extra storage space – it still has to be organized to be useful. This means the area still needs decluttering and ordering – and for you to stop thinking of it as a dumping ground.

The first step of a garage clear-out is to gather everything together that can be binned and box or bag it up to be taken to the tip. Then gather everything that can be donated to a good home and do the same. Finally, you'll be left with all the things you actually want to keep and now is the time to get them in piles, according to type, ready to be tucked away into their rightful place.

A well-organized garage should be divided up into areas dedicated to specific tasks and themes, for example tools, bikes, sports equipment, garden furniture and lawn care.

Arrange it so that frequently used items are easily accessible, while seasonal items such as sledges and beach chairs are placed in a separate storage area that's harder to reach.

Maximize vertical space on the garage walls with some sturdy shelving systems for larger items.

# #94
# OUTGROWN OUTDOOR TOYS

---------------------------------

Once your kids are older, then it's time to get rid of those outdoor swing sets, climbing frames and water slides – all of which take up substantial space in your garden. Not to mention all those balls and rackets and plastic garden games. Anything that is still in good enough shape can go to a good home – perhaps even someone on your street.

# #95
## FIND OUT WHERE TO DISPOSE OF GARDEN WASTE

----------------------------------

For all the stuff you can't repurpose, get clued up on what your local council will collect. Most councils will provide you with a separate garden bin or bag for this purpose. Alternatively, you can take garden refuse to your local recycling centre location. Some debris can be incinerated on a home bonfire – but do check the council website for any guidelines – while a home composter will eventually turn both garden and food waste into useful fertilizer.

# #96
## RESPECT YOUR REMAINING STUFF

---------------------------------

The best way to avoid constantly acquiring new tools, furniture and plants is to take better care of the ones you already have. Treat possessions with respect, which means cleaning tools, sharpening blades, storing summer furniture safely in the winter months, and watering and feeding plants. You don't have to be green-fingered; you just need to show living things some love and attention.

# KEEPING
# IT UP